A Fugitive's Daughter

Vikkiana Fernandez

Editor: Sharp Editorial, LLC

Publisher: Chynna Creative Co., LLC

DEDICATION

This book is dedicated to my father and my fiancé.

Table of Contents

ACKNOWLEDGEMENTS

A big thanks to my father, who inspired me and gave me permission and the privilege to write this book based on his life and the crazy experiences he faced over the last 17 years. I also want to acknowledge my soon-to-be husband, for pushing me and encouraging me to write this book and giving me the constant motivation I needed to write this deeply personal novel. Thank you, God, for giving me the courage to write this book and always letting me know that the only way I will fail is if I don't try. I would also like to thank my publisher, Chynna Denny for seeing this project through to its final stage. Last, but certainly not least, I would like to thank Laci Swann, my editor, for making this possible.

INTRODUCTION

"Courage doesn't always roar. Sometimes courage is the little voice at the end of the day that says I'll try again tomorrow."
– Mary Anne Radmacher

This day was different, unlike the countless other days I walked home from school. Very different, to say the least. Usually, around this time of day, I would walk home and feel happy and relieved that the school day has come to an end. Normally, I had homework to do, but I knew once I finished that up, I could play outside with friends until the streetlights came on. The joys of childhood, right? On this day, though, I woke up feeling anxious, and I was on pins and needles throughout the morning and afternoon regarding how the next 24 hours would pan out. So, when the school bell rang to signify the end of the day, and I started heading home, I knew

I wasn't about to walk into our home for an after-school snack before starting my homework. Although I didn't know what to expect, I wasn't necessarily expecting the worst, either. Needless to say, this day was anything but normal, especially for an 11-year-old. At that age, one's biggest concern should be vocabulary words or convincing their parents to play outside later than usual, but on this day, over 15 years ago, my concern was my father's potential jail sentence, as he was to appear at the courthouse regarding his drug trafficking charges.

As I approached our front door, my stomach tightened into a million knots. I was steps away from walking into our home to greet my mother and discover my father's verdict. In retrospect, my heart aches for the 11-year-old version of myself, because I was dealing with something no child should have to face. Nevertheless, that's life, and we deal with the cards we are dealt with.

As for my mom, I knew that her mind was racing as well. That day wasn't exactly easy for any of us, especially her. When I left for school that morning, she gave me a hug and a smile, like she always does, but I felt her spirit, and she was unsettled. I imagine I would feel the same if I knew my man was facing serious jail time.

Taking a deep breath and walking through the front door, I saw my mom on the couch with my brother and immediately knew something was wrong. Mom's face was puffy from crying, and the tears continued to flow as she sat on the couch, seemingly lifeless, in our living room.

"Mom, what happened to my dad? I timidly asked, afraid to further upset her but dying to know what was going on with my father.

My mom looked at me with tears in her eyes and finally gave a few short replies to my question. Within moments, I was shocked to learn that my father was on the run, now wanted by law enforcement. Reality quickly hit like a ton of bricks, and although I understood what my mother had said, I remained confused, questioning whether this was my life or a bad dream because I couldn't fathom my father leaving home for good.

Upon discovering that my father left the courthouse with intentions of never looking back was a punch to the gut. Honestly, "a punch to the gut" is putting it mildly. My world crashed, I was petrified, and countless thoughts swirled through my young mind.

Will I ever see my dad again?

Is he safe?

What's going to happen to our family?

How will we survive?

What the hell is going on?

The feeling of having to throw up, shit, cry, and scream hit me at once. I was on a hellish emotional roller coaster with no signs of getting off anytime soon. On that day, the world fell silent, and although my mother and siblings were within arm's reach, I felt alone, kind of like a dramatic movie scene, but this was no movie. This was my life.

I soon learned that by the time school ended that day, my dad was already long gone. Where, I wasn't sure, but he was gone. Very little was said to me that afternoon, and my mom's explanation was not exactly elaborate. Assumedly, her shock and sadness, combined with the fact that I was only 11 years old, held my mom back from divulging details about Dad's whereabouts. Plus, there wasn't much to share. He was on the run, and no one knew the ins and outs of his status.

Eight short hours before this hellish nightmare, I saw my father, as I did every morning. Before I left for school, I had walked downstairs to the basement where my dad was praying, something he did every day. I kissed him on the cheek and told him I loved him. My dad appeared nervous, and his energy was... *off*. This was unusual because my father was an even-keel kind of guy. After giving him a kiss, I walked upstairs, and my siblings and I went off to school. From that point forward, I had a weird feeling in my stomach because I knew my father had a court appearance that morning, and his anxious demeanor put me on edge. Then again, what did I know? I was just a young girl who, hours later, came face-to-face with a reality she had no idea how to handle. At such a tender age, my intuition was on par with someone with many more years under their belt. I had a nervous feeling in my stomach for a reason. The gut never lies.

That morning, my father went to the courthouse. He was supposed to be there by 8:30 a.m. to meet his lawyer. However, for whatever reason, the judge needed to push back my father's hearing for a few hours. So, my father was to meet his lawyer at the courthouse a couple of hours later. My father never returned to that courthouse, though. Instead, he fled, leaving behind his wife, kids, and the only life he knew.

***

My name is Vikkiana Fernandez, and this is my story. Well, this is my father's story, told through the eyes of me, his daughter, a woman who has nothing but unconditional love for her dad when many might question why. My journey is unique and seemingly unbelievable, but this is my truth. Never in a million years would I have thought that my dad, the man I love with everything in my heart and soul, was a big-time drug dealer. More shockingly, I never thought he would end up living a life on the run. My father was a fugitive for 17 years, and each step of the way could easily be a scene from the most intense action-drama movie you could ever imagine. My father's decision to sell drugs and then flee from his court-ordered hearing forced him to give up on his lady and his family to save himself from time behind bars and possible deportation. Although he chose himself in the heat of the moment, he believed his risky decision would save our family in the long run.

What would you have done if you were him?

That is a question I ask myself nearly every day, and every day I can't quite come to a definitive answer. I pray I never have to face that situation, and I hope those circumstances do not find their way into my life, either. Then again, I live a relatively normal life with my family, so a life on the run isn't something I would have to contemplate.

Some may have folded if they were in my father's position. Some may have gone crazy, and some may have experienced denial. Until that moment plays out, who really knows how one would react? What I do know is that although I had some wild-ass coming-to-life moments throughout the last several years, I ultimately realized that this story, my life and my father's run from the law, serves very deep and purposeful lessons, lessons that molded me into the woman I am today. Between God working in mysterious ways, to understanding the harsh truth that nothing lasts forever, plus coming to grips with the fact that you should never judge a book by its cover, the Lord brought me to a place of understanding in dealing with and reflecting on my life as well as how to shy away from judging others, something people seemingly do without hesitation.

"I would never do anything like that!"

"How could he put himself in that position?"

"What a selfish person."

"Who would ever do that?"

Amid this chaotic experience, I learned invaluable lessons, one of which involves judgment. It's very easy and almost natural to tell someone how you would handle a problem or what you would do if you were in their shoes, but you never really know until you're in the position. I've heard it all, whether people knew I caught wind of their harsh judgments, and although I would probably wonder some of those same questions if the shoe was on the other foot, I'm asking you not to be so quick to judge my dad or write him off. He's most certainly aware of his part and subsequent impact in this ordeal. Every action has a reaction, and it came to no surprise to my father that the reaction from everyone affected was devastation. He knows he fucked up and he knows he made poor decisions, and although he didn't pay his consequences in prison, he paid the price alone – lonely holidays, living in fear, constant paranoia and looking over his shoulder, late-night cries, being so close yet so far from his loved ones, and no access to medical treatment when he needed it most. There was no cold drink in one hand with a book in the other while he sat on an island and chuckled about dodging the law. In fact, my father's circumstances were quite the opposite.

Despite the pain, confusion, and unfamiliar territory we had walked throughout my father's time on the run, I wholeheartedly believe that God made no mistakes, not then and not now. Everyone's story is already written before we are in the womb, so although my father physically journeyed alone, God never left his side or mine. My father's faith grew immeasurably, as did mine, and his story is a true testament to faith, not because he was never caught but because I stayed prayed up and deeply faithful despite disappointments, uncertainty, sadness, and chaos. That signifies victory that I never let the enemy reign supreme. God remained ever-present, and I am eternally grateful for His mercy and grace, especially during my father's tumultuous time on the run.

My father's decisions affected my life in a major way, so much so that my wisdom and understanding regarding life developed profoundly at a young age. In learning about yourself, you often want to share your newfound wisdom with others, and my hope is that you not only gain a deep look into my life but that my life lessons help you as you walk on your journey, too. If anything, whether you gain insight or learn a valuable lesson, the story of my father's life on the run is mind-blowing, so you will at least enjoy a wild tale of a man I know and love.

CHAPTER ONE

"Better to be a strong man with a weak point, than to be a weak man without a strong point. A diamond with a flaw is more valuable than a brick without a flaw."
– William J. H. Boetcker

I am the third-born child to my Puerto Rican mother and the first-born child to my Dominican father. I was born in the small city of Reading, Pennsylvania, back in 1991, and raised in a strict household yet never needed for a thing. My parents were strict about chores, doing well in school, and being on my best behavior, yet they spoiled the hell out of us. Our lives in Reading, Pennsylvania, back in the 90s, are night and day compared to the life I live today. No longer the little girl with very few cares in the world, I am now a 28-year-old fiancé and mother of five beautiful children, three girls, and two boys.

We have a full house!

My wonderful partner and I work incredibly hard to provide a stable, loving life for our family. We take pride in putting food on the table, a safe and comfortable roof over our kids' heads, and sweet luxuries our kids will remember forever, such as dinners out, camps in the summer, and fun holiday vacations. I consider myself a serial entrepreneur, and I attribute my strong ambition to my father, a man who always stayed on his grind. Granted, our grinds were different, but my drive always mirrored his drive. All in all, our lives are peaceful, joyful, and maybe even a bit boring to some, but after all I've been through, boring is good, really good.

Growing up, the stability factor in my mother and father's home was considerably different than the home that my partner and I have created. The love in my parents' home and relationship was always there, without question, but due to my father's job, we experienced a different lifestyle that subjected our family to an unconventional mode of living than anyone we happened to know. While most children can recall their parents coming home around dinner time after eight hours of work, my dad came and went at odd hours. Nevertheless, that was our norm, and I never needed or wanted for anything because my father was making a living from drug trafficking.

At the time, I had no idea what he was up to, but what I did know was that our family was secure and never went without. As a young girl, I didn't put much thought into anything else because there was food on the table, toys in my toy chest, and happy faces in our home. Maybe if I were older, I would've put more thought into our situation, but if anything, I believe my parents shielded me from a lot and let me live my childhood in a carefree way. My dad, though, was trafficking heroin and cocaine to make this carefree life happen. I thought his job involved working with lawyers, and when he was gone at night, I assumed he enjoyed hanging out with his friends. When he would leave for other cities and states, I figured he was visiting family and friends. I mean, I was a child. I didn't put deep thought into potential truths and lies. I took his word at face value. I didn't dissect his schedule or whereabouts. As a young girl, my cares were friends, candy, and toys. Anything else was off my radar, especially because the drugs weren't around. Our life may have been like a movie, but we didn't have a table full of coke or heroin being divided into bags on the kitchen counter. These drugs were completely out of sight.

***

My father was born in the capital of the Dominican Republic. When he was nine years old, he and his family migrated to Puerto Rico, where he lived until his early 20s. My father had big dreams, so he attended a four-year college in Rio Piedras to earn a degree in hopes of moving closer to his dream of working in finance. He wanted to be an accountant, a far cry from a drug trafficker, I know. He got through all four years of college yet didn't take his finals because he thought it would be a better idea to move to New York City and get rich. You know, the typical American dream – move to the Big Apple and make it big.

In 1982, he left Puerto Rico and made his grand entrance to New York City, where he went to visit a friend to determine whether his plan would pan out for the long run. My father didn't have a detailed plan, but his dreams were fueled by his love for the fast life – salsa dancing until sunrise, a city that doesn't sleep, and countless options for work. After only a few days, he decided to stay. He sold clothes on 176 & St. Nicholas in Manhattan. This job didn't pay a lot, and it wasn't his dream job, but it helped him get by in the meantime. He and his friend eventually decided to leave New York and start fresh somewhere else. So, they took all the money they had, hopped in the car, and decided to drive until the gas ran out. Wherever that might be is where they would decide to stay. Well, the gas ran out in Reading, Pennsylvania, a city neither of them ever heard of but figured it was worth a try because they had nothing to lose. As an adult, I learned more about my father, and I realized my dad had always been a risk-taker. He was willing to risk a lot, and he seemed to throw his fear to the wind.

My father and his friend rented a two-bedroom apartment, and everything was good until the money they had started running low. However, one night at the club, everything changed, and they no longer had to worry about staying financially afloat. They met some people who were in the drug business, and those people offered to help my dad and his friend get on their feet. My father went to the club for fun, dancing, and drinks, and he left with new connections to a world he was about to dive into, head-first.

Little did my father know, his life was about to change forever and not just for the time being.

In very little time, my dad and his friend started selling heroin on the streets of Bethlehem, Pennsylvania, and the money was pouring in. In fact, the money got so good that they rented a house in Bethlehem so that they could stash their shit and not have to drive back and forth with so much illegal material. Their home in Bethlehem wasn't some typical trap house, either. This was a beautiful, three-bedroom house with a pool and garage. When Bethlehem started getting "hot," and the drug scene became more prominent, Dad and his friend decided to leave the house and stay low in Reading for a while.

One night, my father decided to head to the club again, this time to enjoy a fun night out. Might I add – my dad is very well-known, everywhere he steps foot, for his astonishing salsa dancing skills. He will dance circles around you and throw down some moves that will keep you dazed.

"Dancing makes me feel alive," my dad would say, and I could see the twinkle in his eyes as he shared his love for salsa.

When my father was at the club that night, he met my mother, and they immediately hit it off. Apparently, the club scene always brought my father much more than a night of shots and dancing — first, an introduction to the drug scene. Next, an introduction to my beautiful mother. When he met my mom, he was honest about what he did for a living, but she wasn't about that life, so my father kept the drugs away from her. She knew what he was doing, but she wanted no parts of it. So, he always kept his "business" separate from their relationship. Some may wonder why she agreed to get involved with him, and that's not something I can judge. They had a connection, and it was undeniable. The heart often overrules the mind.

Nevertheless, she turned a blind eye to his "profession." His lifestyle had no bearing on the way he treated my mom. Some may believe a drug trafficker has a cold heart or doesn't know how to love, but my dad truly treated my mom like royalty. He adored her, spoiled her, and loved her deeply. She was his pride and joy, and everyone could easily see the love between them. From date nights to his affectionate nature to the thought he put into every surprise he gifted her, big and small, he treated my mom with nothing but the utmost love and respect.

Because my father was already dealing drugs before he met my mom, he continued with his venture, despite my mom's disdain toward the business. Before their relationship, my father had already decided to expand his enterprise to Lancaster and Allentown as well as Hartford, New Haven, and Waterbury, Connecticut.

He didn't stop there, though.

He expanded to Long Island, Brockton, Boston, a few cities in Ohio, and many other cities in the north. His business was massive, and so was his influence. He broke bread with everyone in his circle and beyond, and you could say with certainty that my father did not have a selfish bone in his body. He was a leader, a man who showed respect for everyone, no exceptions.

About seven months after my mom and dad met, she got pregnant with little ol' me, and as she was pregnant with me, my dad's mistress was also pregnant.

Yeah, that part.

With the fast life comes instability in other areas besides the work environment. My father had a mistress, and his life wasn't just awry in terms of drugs. His love life was, too. It seems contradictory to mention how much my father loved and respected my mom when he had a mistress, but in typical fast-life fashion, women flocked to money and power.

One night, at a club on 8th and Franklin, my dad met his soon-to-be mistress through one of his friends. My father also discovered that this woman didn't live too far from our home, which soon led to the conception of my sister. When Dad's mistress found out she was pregnant, she told my dad that she was keeping the baby. Dad wasn't happy with her decision, but everything truly happens for a reason because I can't imagine life without my sister. When my mom discovered that my dad had a pregnant mistress, she wasn't happy, not at all, but her heart changed, too, because my sister soon became part of our family. Apparently, in the heat of an argument with my father, my father's mistress angrily told my mom that she was pregnant with my father's child. From there, my mom had a decision – stay or leave. She stayed, not exactly happily, but she stuck around, and from there, she had a change of heart – not toward the mistress but the innocent child in all of this, my sister.

Mom gave birth to me in 1991, and my sister was born

shortly after that in 1992. My sister and I are only seven months apart, so I guess you could say we are Irish twins... kind of. Before the argument between my mom and father's mistress, Mom had no idea Dad was hoeing around, but my sister's mom knew he had a wifey. She didn't care, though. She was a party animal and she was into the same shit he was – drugs and money. My father could hide drugs at her house and do what he wanted, but my father knew better than to bring that shit home to my mom. My father managed to live a double life, most men can't take care of one woman and my dad managed to take care of two at one time.

To share how much Dad loved Mom yet discuss Dad's mistress in the same breath is a strange feeling, but that's not for me to make sense of or justify. That is part of his story, and every story isn't necessarily a page from a fairy tale. With Dad's line of work came temptations, circumstances, and influences that other adults may not face or come in contact with, and although my father had a choice as to whether he would cheat, he took a path I'm sure he wishes he could reverse and reroute.

As his lust for money grew, my father continued to expand his business, and he eventually became a global drug dealer. In 1995, he picked up the cocaine flow. Back then, people were using that shit like oxygen. The way people chain-smoke cigarettes pales in comparison to the way people abused cocaine. My father knew that the cocaine market was untapped in our area, so he pursued distributing cocaine with no qualms. Drugs are a business, a scary business at that, but like other types of legal companies, there are factors to assess and analyze. My father knew these factors, and he moved accordingly, which led to a great deal of wealth. His business acumen was unparalleled.

The money was pouring in, and my parents realized they would need a legal means to wash this continual illegal cash flow. So, in 1996, they decided to open a bodega in Reading, Pennsylvania. One of my most vivid memories of that store was when my brother and I were sitting on an ice cream cooler as my mom tended to the front. Suddenly, some piece of shit busted through the door like a bat out of hell, with a knife, demanding money and cigarettes. Despite my brother and I sitting there, wide-eyed and afraid, the thief put his knife to my mom's neck, careless of the two sets of young eyes on him. My mom quickly turned around, and in one swoop, she grabbed the knife, broke it in half and said, "You will not do this in front of my kids." The unknown man sprinted from the bodega and never returned. That was such a scary moment, but it showed me so much about my mom. She had the strength to break that knife and the courage to stand up to that man.

Despite the bodega venture being a legal means to earn and funnel money, you can't live an illegal life and expect it to last forever. The streets talk, and when you're not living right, the truth eventually comes to light. Well, the man who sold my dad the bodega got caught up with the cops. He was doing illegal shit, too. So, he cooperated with authorities, ultimately telling them my dad was a dealer. In turn, the cops raided our home. They turned our house upside down. Thankfully, my brother and I were at school at the time of the raid. I was five years old, and my brother was eight, so I'm grateful we weren't home to see that because I'm sure it would've been permanently embedded in our minds. My mom and aunt were at the house though.

The cops found 54 grams of cocaine, hardly anything compared to what Dad was regularly pushing, but I suppose this was left behind at our house as my dad carted the stuff back and forth to his stash house. When the detectives found the cocaine, they immediately apprehended my mom and aunt. My dad was on his way back from New York after picking up a couple of kilos, and when he called home and no one answered, he felt that something was wrong. He had a Corvette Rx 7 at the time, and he had parked it in a garage on Route 61. This was where he dropped off his kilos. My dad sped home and when he was about to approach the house, he saw a commotion outside. So, he kept driving. I figure we all do dumb shit when we get scared, and that included my dad driving past the house. In retrospect, that was the best decision at the time because things could've gotten worse had he entered the home.

That night, Dad was a nervous wreck, and he didn't know what to do. My father ended up at his mistress's sister's house to get his mind right. He knew he was going to take the fall and go to jail because he would never let my mom suffer the consequences, especially for something she had no hand in.

The next day, Dad went to the city hall and turned himself in. In return, the authorities let my mom and aunt go. My father hired a lawyer, but after his lawyer received $10,000 from my father, he then said he did not believe my dad could beat his case. So, my parents fired him. My father's bail was extremely expensive, a fee my dad did not want to pay, especially if it meant sitting in jail for a few months. Instead, he decided to eat the cost. So, my dad told my mom to wait until his bail decreased, hopefully within the next few weeks. However, he sat in jail for 18 months without being sentenced. I was devastated. I cried often and after every phone call and visit.

One of the visits remains fresh in my mind as if it were yesterday that I walked through the doors of the Berks County Prison.

"Everything is going to be okay," my mom had said, reassuring me that the visit would go smoothly, and it would feel good to see my dad.

As we walked through the metal detectors, the correction officer then walked us back to the block to see Dad. A few moments later, my dad walked in our direction, and he was using crutches due to arthritis in his legs. At that moment, I broke down. I sobbed my heart out, and I yet again realized I had no control over my dad, his health, or his jail sentence.

Eventually, his bail was lowered, and all he needed to pay was $6,000. So, my mom hired a new lawyer. At that point, my father's father, my grandpa, came from Puerto Rico and got my pops out of jail (with the help of his newly appointed lawyer.) During Dad's jail stint, he remained out of the drug game for over 18 months, obviously unable to handle any transactions yet not quite willing to let anyone else take control. Thus, our family's finances and stream of income changed dramatically. To alleviate financial stress from my mother, my grandfather contributed money to my dad's attorney fees, and this was the start of Dad's legal proceedings regarding his sentence.

CHAPTER TWO

"Only those who went hungry with me and stood by me when I went through a bad time at some point in life will eat at my table."

– Pablo Escobar

My parents became close friends with my father's lawyer, so much so that when my dad got out of jail, my parents were fortunate to start working with him. Mind you, my father looked, dressed, and acted professionally. At first glance, you'd think Dad was the lawyer.

My parents would bring clients to their lawyer, and the lawyer would pay them a percentage of what he charged his clients. Despite their new legal careers, my dad couldn't stay away from that easy money for too long. By day, Dad had a legal job, and by night, he was back to dealing drugs. Never in my life would I have thought that my dad was the candy man, but I can't complain because when he returned home from jail, life went back to normal. Once again, we had everything we wanted, needed, and then some. Anything I asked for, I got, and my siblings received the same treatment as well, yet we were spoiled in ways far more profound than tangible gifts. Our house was full of love. We weren't perfect, but our love was undeniable. We were a happy family. Our family was close-knit, and that is something I pride myself to this day, also instilling the same type of close-knit feeling in our home among our children. My children know that family comes first. They know that their siblings are their best friends, and they know that family should have your back through thick and thin. My children are spoiled with love in the same fashion I was spoiled with love. Ironically, although my dad was mean in the streets, he was a pushover when it came to spoiling us. So, my mom was often the strict parent.

Oh, the irony.

We vacationed all the time and have so many wonderful memories as kids. Although he lived a crazy life, my father was all about family. In fact, every Sunday was a family day. We would wake up, go to church to praise the Lord, and eat after church service. At night, it was ice cream and a movie. Those moments were the best. Although the day he fled stands out in my mind, those Sunday memories hold a special, happy place in my memory bank.

During this time, my aunt had lived with us, too. Well, she was actually my father's cousin, but they were raised as siblings, so we called her our aunt and viewed her as such. She was like a second mother to my siblings and I. She cooked, cleaned, and showed us so much love. In fact, her yellow rice and beans with chicken and pink potato salad were one of my favorite meals she made for us. The potato salad was pink because she would add red beets to it, and that detail always stood out in my mind. My aunt has the hands of an angel, and her food tasted like it was sent from Heaven. Not only was she a fantastic cook, but she always tried to help me when I was in trouble. Plus, she kept many of my secrets and gave me sound advice. Then, there were those times that she would go out for the evening and come home at 2:30 a.m., and my sister and I would wait downstairs for her, just so she could make us pancakes, and she never said no. However, my aunt was also dealing drugs with my dad. My father kept this business within the family. I was fortunate to have a father that loves me and, essentially, two moms who loved me endlessly too.

Despite Dad's impatience to have quick money in his pocket, he is one of the wisest, most intelligent, smooth, courageous, ambitious, and adventurous people you could ever meet. I suppose his adventurous side led him to live on the edge because he knew, deep down, his life wouldn't always be under the radar.

In 2000, my father sold to an undercover officer that was sent by an informant. The sale involved four bags of cocaine at a value of $20 per bag. The officer came back for more, about seven times, but the last time he came around, he asked my dad for a half-ounce, and all red flags went up. Before asking my dad for the half-ounce, this person had only wanted small amounts. My father quickly concluded that this situation was sketchy. After asking for a half-ounce, he then told my dad to come outside and check out all the girls he had in the car. My dad knew if he went outside, it was to take his picture or grab him.

"I'm okay," my dad had nonchalantly said, knowing a set-up was in progress. "I have a woman at home."

The undercover officer didn't come around anymore,

but a month later, the cops picked up my dad as he parked and walked into a random bar. Later that night, my mom received the dreadful collect call from my dad, telling her he needed her to bail him out. The next day, Dad went in front of the judge. The judge must have felt bad for him because my dad limped into the courtroom.

Since the early 90s, Dad experienced pain in his legs, and he's endured this pain for over 20 years. On this day, the judge overseeing his case was familiar with my father's lawyer and saw my dad plenty of times before this instance. Maybe that added to his sympathy factor, I'm not sure, but the judge told my father that when he bails out, he needs to go straight to the hospital and get his arthritis checked. My dad listened to the judge's instructions, as he knew there was something wrong with his body. That day, my father quickly bailed out of jail, posting bail that wasn't nearly as hefty as his prior charge. Dad proceeded to the hospital, following the judge's advice to look into his bodily issues. After leaving the hospital, we packed our bags and left for Washington, D.C., for a week-long vacation. Dad was out on bail for about two years, going back and forth to court due to delayed court hearings and whatnot. We lived life as if he wasn't possibly facing time in jail, which included my dad still selling drugs, still deep in the game.

CHAPTER THREE

"It's a wise man who understands that every day is a new beginning, because boy, how many mistakes do you make in a day? I don't know about you, but I make plenty. You can't turn the clock back, so you have to look ahead."

– Mel Gibson

In May 2002, our lives took a dramatic turn. The day had finally come for my father's court hearing.

"I love you, Dad," I said before I left for school.

"I love you, too," he said, kissing me on the cheek. "I'll see you later."

While my dad was at the courthouse, his lawyer informed him that the judge wouldn't be seeing him until later that afternoon. In the intermittent, his lawyer was trying to find out how much time they wanted to give him. In my father's mind, one day of jail was too many. He had been down that path before and returning to jail was not something he wanted. I guess he should have thought about that before returning to the game but should've, could've, would've. So, my dad left the courthouse that afternoon, went home, picked up $10,000, and called a friend to pick him up. His friend took him to Allentown, where my father lived with his friend for the next five months.

My father was officially on the run.

He trashed his legal papers having to do with his identity, and he bought a new identity for $1,500. He purchased a social security card and birth certificate of someone who passed away many years prior. Acquiring a new identity seems like an impossible feat, but my dad knew many others who needed to do the same. So, a friend of his retrieved the necessary paperwork and Dad's new identity was attained a brief time after that.

The day my dad fled vividly stands out in my mind, and I don't think I'll ever forget when I came home from school to discover my mom and brother crying on the sofa. When my sister and I came home, I quickly assumed Dad was in jail. At the time, my mom was caring for my sister, the child my dad had with his mistress. When she was three years old, my mom took her in and cared for her like her own, something that could not have been easy for my mom, yet she handled the situation as best she could. Of course, my mom was livid about the situation, but she also knew that this child was innocent. Notably, my sister's mom was rather wild, so having her live with us was the best idea at the time. Anyway, at 11 years old, coping with deep feelings of confusion and loss, I didn't know how to deal with my dad's departure properly. I just looked to the ceiling, said "why," and broke down in tears. The man I loved and adored had left me behind, and it wasn't until I saw him again that this pain got any better.

My dad started working under the table, cutting grass with his friend. This was a man who never really had to bust a sweat a day in his life, yet he was now a fugitive and busting his ass to make a buck. After his brief stay in Allentown, my father relocated to New York, where he bounced around for a few years from family member's houses. Ironically, they didn't know he was on the run. They assumed he and my mom were separated and going through problems. He settled for a while in his grandmother's apartment in Washington Heights. There, in Washington Heights, he had to get down and dirty.

For about nine months, he worked for a window company, fixing and installing windows.

Although Dad was on the run, we were miraculously able to see one another. After a few months, once my dad left home, we met in Baltimore, Maryland, at my mom's sister's house. Also, we spoke occasionally on the phone before our first visit. I have no idea if the phones were bugged, but in retrospect, Dad played it safe because our phone calls were very brief. With every phone call, though, I told him I loved him and missed him, and he would assure me that we would see each other soon. I always wondered where he was, but for a long time, I had no idea, and I didn't question it, either. One may think the question would easily present itself, but when your parent has been gone for quite some time, the only thing on your mind is to tell that person how much you love them.

The day arrived when I somewhat found out the reason behind my dad's absence. During one of our times together in Baltimore, I happened to be sitting in the car with my cousin. I needed to grab a few coins from my mom's wallet, and when I began leafing through her pocketbook, I found a newspaper clipping. This clipping had my father's name on it, and it stated where we lived and that my dad was wanted for drugs. I immediately showed this clipping to my cousin, as any kid would probably do. The sheer shock nearly pushed me to speak up about it. I couldn't just tuck the newspaper clipping back into Mom's wallet as if I never saw it. I had to say something.

"I never thought Dad was into shit like this," I had said in total disbelief. "He was always suited up and professional looking. My father was dealing drugs, though," I shockingly recollected.

Some may wonder if I lost respect for him, if I feared him, or maybe even felt disgusted, but I felt none of those emotions. In fact, I really didn't know how I was supposed to feel about my father and the entire situation. Everything happened so fast, and what stood out the most was the sadness I felt and couldn't shake because I could no longer see my dad every day. The little things like kissing him on his cheek before school and talking to him when I came home after playing outside with friends were the things I deeply missed and took for granted. I never realized how those small moments occupied the biggest place in my heart… until I could no longer experience those moments with him.

Now that we were a little more comfortable visiting, I started staying with my dad during the summer. Dad wasn't the only one who had to adjust to dodging the law. We did, too, each time my siblings and I chose to visit him. At 14 years old, I was visiting my dad at my great-grandmother's one-bedroom apartment in Washington Heights, where he was hiding out. Although my father was no longer at our home, and our family days and trips came to an end, I had the time of my life when I stayed with him in New York. It was just him and me, and this one-on-one time was a new experience for us. As a pre-teen, this quality time was so important. These are the years a child becomes more impressionable, and I'm grateful to have had some solo time with my father because it introduced a new level to our father-daughter relationship, one that involved better communication and, of course, love. During these visits, I felt like an only child because my siblings remained at home.

My siblings visited my dad a few times, but I visited the most because I felt a strong need to see my dad every chance I had. That's my dad, and I missed him terribly. My siblings, on the other hand, were older, and my dad wasn't their biological father, except for my sister, and although they grew up around him for most of their lives, their urge to visit him wasn't as strong as mine. My sister, though, was unable to visit because she was in and out of group homes during that time. After my dad left Reading, she became very rebellious, and my mom lost control of her. Between refusing to listen to my mom and running away every chance she got, my sister was unruly. So, my sister ended up running away from a group home that she had stayed at in Reading and then moved to New York when she was 15 years old.

She chose New York because she wanted to be with our dad, especially since she was unable to see him during her stints in group homes. So, she hopped on a door-to-door transportation bus and had a plan to stay with my father, the only place she felt she could turn to at that time.

When my sister arrived in New York, my dad decided to find a place where they could live together. The fear factor was still there in terms of my father getting caught, but as any parent would, he wanted to make sure her needs were tended to, especially because she was going through such a tumultuous time in her life. She was in a bad emotional and mental space, and my dad knew his fleeing had a lot to do with her rebellion. So, they lived together for a while until she was old enough to rent a room elsewhere. During her time in New York, she was wild, and not much had changed since she left Reading, so not only was my father a fugitive on the run but he was living with a wild child. My sister was getting into trouble and doing whatever she wanted, which often didn't involve the best decisions. She made her own rules, and those rules weren't exactly aligned with the law. My dad didn't need the unwanted attention that my sister inevitably attracted, so she moved out on her own. He never kicked her out; she willingly left, but there was only so much my dad could do for her, and they both knew it.

One may have thought my sister would have been devastated about moving on her own, especially as a teenager, but she has always been a true survivor. If you put her in the middle of the woods, alone, she would find her way out, but her age, inexperience with life, and by-any-means-necessary mentality made for a troubled young woman. My parents couldn't control her and I couldn't do much, either. So, I did the only thing I could do – control what was within my control, and that was myself. I seized opportunities with my dad, and I treasured each moment.

During my visits to New York, life felt free yet stable,

the dichotomy of freedom and stability I craved in Reading during his time on the run. Ironically, I also knew freedom and stability weren't exactly the pillar of our lives because I was visiting my fugitive father to whom I could not talk about to others. Still, I felt joy. I could stay out late with my new friends from around the way, and my father would give me some spending money, so I'd walk through Broadway, shopping like I was grown but still knowing my limits. When I visited my father, I quickly discovered that my dad learned how to cook, clean, and live a low-key life, a drastic difference from his fast-paced, lavish life from years past. My father was content, though. He had no other choice, really. This was his new life, and he needed to make the best of it, or his emotions and thoughts would drown him.

During the first night of my first trip to New York, I stood in silence in my great-grandmother's kitchen as I watched my dad cook steak and seafood salad. I was amazed because this was the first time I saw his domestic skills, something my mom and aunt always handled in Reading. His new cooking skills weren't the only thing I noticed. I also noticed he had a new name, and I had to get used to calling him by this name. The funny thing is, my father never told me to call him by his fake name. I always called him "Papi," so I had no reason to call him by any other name. However, I heard people calling him by his new name, and he would respond.

"Papi, do they know your real name?" I had asked him one day.

"No," he replied without further explanation.

I was confused, but I didn't ask any other questions. In time, I got used to it, but the initial adjustment was awkward.

From his new lifestyle to his new name, I was often in a state of adjustment, yet I remained thankful he had a roof over his head. My dad was truly fortunate to have my great-grandmother's home to stay in during this time. My great-grandmother was deceased, but my dad's cousin took over the apartment, and he had allowed my dad to stay there during that time. Actually, my father had the home to himself because his cousin lived elsewhere. His cousin merely managed the apartment. Whether my father's cousin knew he was on the run was unbeknown to me, but he allowed my father to stay there and never said a word to him about needing to leave. I had wished I could live with him but, of course, I couldn't. Visiting was risky enough, so I knew that living together would be damn near impossible. The truth is, we became comfortable with the idea of me visiting him in New York. My mom, dad, and I got used to this, and our fear factor subsided.

Before that summer trip to New York, I had spent many months without seeing my dad, besides the one visit we had in Maryland and only speaking to him here and there on the phone. For a little over a year, detectives came by our house looking for him, and life had really changed for my family and I during that time. The authorities followed my mom, assumedly with hopes to find my father or get an inkling as to where he could be hiding. My mom knew they were watching. She expected it. With time, my dad was able to calm down a bit. After all, he may have remained on the wanted list but there were other fugitives on the rise, too. So, after my dad eased up a little and his paranoia subsided, we met up again in Maryland at my aunt's house, and we went to Myrtle Beach and spent a few days there, too. I looked forward to spending time on the beach with my dad, one of my favorite places with one of my favorite people.

The first time my father and I spoke thoroughly about his situation, I was 13 years old. While on this trip, my father and I took a long walk along the beach. During our walk, he slowly came to a stop after I had asked him a question that had long been on my mind. At this moment, he finally opened up and explained that he was selling drugs for many years and it finally caught up to him. I kicked off the conversation but had no idea my dad would tell me the whole truth.

"Papi, why did you leave?" I had asked my father. I felt my throat tighten up as the words escaped my mouth. I missed him so much, and I just wanted to know why he left.

"Well, your dad did some things he's not proud of and I had to pay the consequences," he explained.

"I don't understand..." I managed to say through tears.

"I was selling drugs, Baby," he said, and I could tell he wished he had a different answer to my question. "They wanted to put me in jail, but I refused to go because if I were charged, I would face deportation. I felt so bad leaving you guys. I feel like a coward, but it's too late – I've been on the run for a while, and it is what it is at this point."

Still confused, I looked at my father and told him I loved him.

There is an unexplainable love and loyalty one feels toward their family, especially their parents, and nothing he could have said at that moment would have diminished my love for him. To those on the outside, this may seem hard to understand or unfathomable, but this is a feeling that's very real and, at the same time, confusing. I knew my father did wrong, but I loved him anyway. As kids and young adults, we easily forget that our parents are human. They mess up, they make mistakes, and they're still growing, even as adults. As a parent, I realize this truth more than ever, because although I'm in a good place in life, I'm constantly evolving and growing, sometimes due to my mistakes. So, at that moment, I saw a new side to my father. He was still a superhero in my eyes, but I saw his vulnerability.

With watery eyes, my father looked at me and said, "I love you, too, Mi Vida."

At this point, I felt better about having to hold this big secret that weighed so heavily on my shoulders because I had a bit more information and some clarity on why I couldn't tell anyone that I see and speak to my dad. Imagine being a young girl, knowing that if you ever tell anyone that your dad is a fugitive and you know where he is and talk to him all the time, that he could face major jail time. Of course, I did not want my dad in jail, so I kept quiet. I knew that I never wanted to be the reason my dad got caught, so I vowed never to say a word about his whereabouts. Even though his secret weighed heavily on my mind and heart, I felt excited about living a secret life. I mean, I was a strait-laced teenager who now had some drama in her life. I would get on the bus to see my dad, and we were different people during our times together because no one around us knew who we were nor did they know our real identities. So, from that day forward, the day my dad told me the truth, he always kept it real with me, and I appreciated his honesty. Nevertheless, the worst part of seeing him was knowing I had to go home and leave him alone.

CHAPTER FOUR

"A single conversation across the table with a wise man is better
than ten years mere study of books."

– Henry Wadsworth Longfellow

Dad continued to work and live life in New York. His options were limited, and that was the life he needed to get accustomed to because it was the only life he could live while on the run. For my dad, life on the run involved a lot of looking over his shoulders, minding his p's and q's, and avoiding any situation or place that may attract unwanted attention.

In 2004, on a brutally hot summer day in Manhattan, my dad stopped inside his favorite barbershop. Suddenly, a brawl erupted outside the shop, and my dad tried to quietly make his way out before the cops arrived. Well, the cops approached the scene in the blink of an eye, broke up the fight, and started arresting everyone, including my dad.

If he could have shit out his heart, he would have, because according to my father, he was more afraid than ever.

In fact, he was petrified, trying his best to explain to the cops that he was just coming out of the barbershop and had no idea of what was going on, but they didn't want to hear it. The cops took my father to the precinct on 170th and Audubon, where they held him for two days, and all he could think of is how the hell he would manage to get out of this mess. He feared they would find out he was a fugitive from Pennsylvania. However, the strangest part of this ordeal is that when they asked for his identification he gave the fake ID and nothing happened. Perhaps the situation was chaotic, or maybe the officers weren't as strict or regimented as they are today, I don't know, but what I do know is that they never figured out that he was a fugitive. I know my dad wasn't perfect, but it was as if he always had angels watching over him because he had countless run-ins that could've led to his demise, but nothing ever unfolded. It's unreal to think that no one looked further into his identity or demanded his side of the story or an eye-witness account.

The following Monday morning, my father was

escorted to New York County Criminal Court to see a judge. Despite his anxiety, my dad is a very religious man, and he knows that God works in mysterious ways. Before my dad's life on the run, he was adamant about attending church every Sunday, not for routine's sake but because he wanted us to worship our Father. My parents made sure we experienced our first communion, too, and through these spiritual experiences and regular Sunday sermons, we learned about God in a very personal manner.

"Leave your worries in God's hands."

"God is good all the time, and all the time, God is good."

"He forgives us, no matter what."

"God already wrote your story. You're just playing it out."

My father said those statements time and time again, from the moment I was old enough to remember to this very day. I grew up knowing that I was never too busy to thank God, to pray when in need, pray to give thanks, and worship Him no matter the circumstances. Well, the day my father was escorted to court, a well-known attorney showed up for my dad, and my dad was so confused, wondering who the hell this guy was and why he was defending him. The attorney told my dad someone paid him to show up in his defense because they explained my dad had nothing to do with that fight. The attorney spoke with the judge, and they let my dad go, the judge inevitably threw the case out. To this day, my dad has no idea who paid that attorney. Talk about dodging a bullet.

CHAPTER FIVE

"He is a wise man who does not grieve for the things which he has
not but rejoices for those which he has."

– Epictetus

After my father's case was dismissed, he showed up at his attorney's office and asked him if he could work for him because he had the experience needed to pull in more clients. The attorney gladly agreed, and my father immediately began his new job with his former attorney.

Keep in mind, my father can only say about five words in English. He understands more than he can speak, yet he has always managed to get by. When my sister and I were kids, he would pay us to go with him and clients to the courthouse and translate for him, and we made some good money, might I add.

Anyways, with my dad's new gig, he would sit outside the courtrooms for hours, giving out business cards in hopes of bringing in some clients. Soon enough, he started gaining a lot of clients and getting his money up in the process, which was a win-win for my father and his former attorney. In the process of my dad's legal hustle, much of which required standing on his feet for long periods, his body began reacting negatively. His gout, which is a form of arthritis, was becoming progressively worse. His fingers, knees, feet, and elbows were affected and becoming deformed. However, he was unable to seek medical attention because that would require showing identification, and although he had identification, that didn't mean he wanted to use it freely because the person on the card and subsequent paperwork was not him.

Before my dad's arrival in New York, when he first left on the run, he went to a botanica, a place where a person can go to get cleansed or have their cards read. The woman at the botanica said something very powerful to my father.

"I'm going to tell you two things," she said, "and if you follow them, you won't have any more run-ins with the law. No matter how hot it is outside, always dress in a suit and tie because the cops won't stop you if you look like a businessman. The second thing is this – never go to the hospital with that fake identity."

My father kept that advice in the back of his head, refusing to step foot inside a hospital or medical facility, no matter the reason.

Dressing in a suit and tie was nothing for my dad. Since he was a young boy, my dad has always dressed in suits and ties because my grandfather was a tailor in Puerto Rico. So, he always made sure my dad, uncle, and aunt looked good. You could never tell that my father was once a drug dealer or that he was struggling without a penny in his pocket because he always looked like a million bucks. My father took heed to her advice, and his worsening gout was not going to change his mind, either.

CHAPTER SIX

"Smile from your heart; nothing is more beautiful than a woman who is happy to be herself."

– Kubra Sait

Growing up without my dad in our home was so different from the life I once knew as a little girl. With my dad's drug trafficking days behind him, and as he lived miles away from us, my mom had to go to work to provide for my siblings and me. So, she started working as a bartender, and that's when my sister and I became wild. No longer the strait-laced pre-teen I once was, I grew into a teenager who ran the streets at night while my mom worked. My sister and I thought we were the shit, out there smoking weed and cigarettes and trying other stupid shit like e-pills, everything we had no business doing at our age. I'm certainly not proud of the decisions I made, and I most definitely wasn't a good example for my sister, but this was our reality at the time. Sadly, my aunt was no longer living with us, so her once-powerful influence was now nonexistent.

Before we started running wild, my aunt got caught up with the cops and was deported to the Dominican Republic. The combination of my mom's work hours and the lack of other adult figures in the house added to our decision to run wild. My sister and I had more freedom, fewer rules, and very little structure when no one was home. We could have made better decisions, despite our circumstances, but we didn't. You live and you learn. In retrospect, I was doing all that dumb stuff to get lost in my thoughts. From skipping school and smoking weed to staying out until all hours of the night, I was doing everything in my power to escape reality. The sporadic, short trips to New York to visit my dad were not enough to quiet the pain inside from his permanent absence, especially as I returned to life in Reading without him. Worse, when you run the streets at night, you usually don't make the most sound-minded friends, and the company I kept was not exactly the best.

When I was 14 years old, I lost my virginity to a guy that

I thought I was deeply in love with, but I suppose everyone thinks their first is "the one." I had no business having sex at the age or carelessly throwing around the phrase "I love you," either. However, when someone tells you they love you, you believe it because it sounds good, especially at the impressionable age of 14. It sounds like a teenage fairy tale, but let me tell you – this was no fairy tale. That guy put me through hell at a young age, namely physical abuse.

There was an incident when he suddenly started to choke me on my cousin's neighbor's porch, and when his hands were gripping my neck, all I could do was look him in the face and wonder why he wanted to hurt me. I was devastated and afraid. As he was choking me, my cousin came running out of the house.

"Get off of her!" she shouted at the top of her lungs as he reluctantly released his grip on my neck.

After that dreaded day, he didn't apologize, not right away, at least. He made it seem as though the situation was my fault, shifting the blame to me, and I was so blinded by "love" that I stayed because I believed it was my fault and that it wouldn't happen again. Sadly, he didn't have to manipulate me to stay because I gave myself a laundry list of reasons as to why we should be together and why I shouldn't stop dating him.

The choking turned into a punch, and there came a time, soon after that, when my boyfriend struck me in the lip. At this point, sadly, I was no longer afraid, but I was in shock that he continued to take his abuse to new heights. That particular time, unlike before, I had the courage to defend myself and punch him in the eye. Immediately after I hit him, I yelled for my sister and we ran about three blocks from where the incident happened. I had then stopped a random man on the street and asked him if I could use his phone. He was hesitant but eventually agreed. So, I called my mom and waited for her at a nearby store.

To this day, I'm grateful I didn't let fear or shame stop me from seeking my mom's help. When she picked me up, Mom made it known she was furious. She didn't like that I had a "friend" in the first place. My Mom refused to acknowledge him as my boyfriend. Furthermore, my busted lip put her in a rage.

"Stay the fuck away from him!" she demanded at the top of her lungs the second I opened her car door.

Without saying a word, I nodded my head in

agreement. I had enough of his abuse and our toxic merry-go-round of a relationship, and my mom didn't have to tell me twice to stay away.

At that time, I was walking around with a busted, swollen lip, and although those incidents were a bit frightening, I'm eternally grateful I didn't stick around for more because more abuse was inevitable. From that moment forward, I vowed never to let a man put his hands on me again. Although I was making horrible decisions at the time, I dared to walk away from an abusive relationship. Without my father around and my mom working odd hours to provide, I could have stayed with that boy for the sake of companionship. I imagine that's how I would have justified staying. I give God all the praise for exiting that destructive relationship. Although my ex-boyfriend put his hands on me, he did not have the power to take my inner strength. I've always been a smart girl, but I made a lot of poor choices during those formidable years. Again, you live and you learn.

In July of 2007, as I entered the thick of my teenage years, I met a man who ended up being my fiancé and the father of my five children. At the time, however, I would have never known I was staring at the face of my forever love. I met him through a friend when we were hanging out at my friend's house. Our relationship was completely platonic. He and I hung out with our friends, and we did things as a group. His disposition was serious, and he was far from my type in basically every way. He always looked so pensive, whereas I was carefree and always looking to laugh and have fun. Well, after a few months of hanging out, he started to grow on me, and I started to fall for him. It's like they say — opposites attract. After my 16th birthday, we started dating — November 26th, 2007, to be exact. Twelve years later, we remain more in love than ever and I am thankful he is the man who made me a mother and fiancé. He accepted me, flaws and all.

When I met him, I had my guard up. Admittedly, I was deeply broken. I had low self-esteem and was willing to throw in the towel for any little thing, meaning I voluntarily buckled to people and situations that did not serve me well, but this man was the opposite of the abusive person I dated in the past. He was a gentle giant and incredibly loving and kind, but he would fuck up anyone when it came to me. This man was attentive, patient, and all about me. He was a true gentleman, and I not only had fun with him, but I felt safe, too, a feeling that had been robbed from me in the past.

In October of 2008, I found out we were expecting. It was a surprise to us both. Come to think of it, this pregnancy should not have come as a surprise because we were having relations for a few months. However, after months of messing around, I assumed I couldn't have kids because we had yet to become pregnant. Plus, he already had two children, so I knew conception wasn't an issue in terms of his sperm. I was turning 17 the following month, still a baby in age yet mentally older than my peers. I had endured a tumultuous home life due to my father's lifestyle, an absentee parent, an abusive boyfriend, and several other life-changing experiences, so I didn't view a baby as another obstacle or issue. I saw this child as a blessing and a priceless gift. Granted, I was young, but I welcomed motherhood and felt strongly about being a loving, responsible parent. Understandably, many young women my age may feel differently, and their parents would more than likely feel devastated by teenage pregnancy, but this situation was something I knew I could handle. I realize this isn't a typical reaction of a teenager, but my pregnancy was another sign from God that He created me with strength, intention, and a nurturing spirit, and I had every intention of sharing those gifts with our baby.

My mom was the one who bought me the pregnancy test. In fact, she bought me the test when she caught wind that my period was late. After I took the test, and it showed up positive, I walked out of the bathroom, nervously laughing, and handed her my pregnancy test. After Mom saw the outcome, she looked at me and appeared upset, as if she knew I should not be pregnant at such a young age. She looked at the test twice and I couldn't stop laughing not because it was funny but because my nerves were so uncontrollable and she took the test and slapped me in the forehead with it. Moments later, she walked into my bedroom, where my boyfriend was sitting. She looked at him and sternly asked, "Do you plan on taking care of this baby?"

"Yes, ma'am," he quickly replied.

"I pray you do," she said, looking him in the eyes.

Then, Mom gathered her car keys, instructed us to get in the car, and informed us we were going to my boyfriend's mom's house to tell her the news. Mom wasn't exactly jumping for joy, but I could sense a slight feeling of peace regarding my news.

As for my father, I decided to tell him the good news in person. So, I planned a trip to New York. We were at El Valle, a Dominican restaurant on Jerome Avenue in the Bronx when I revealed the news. Upon hearing my announcement, my dad rubbed his hand across his chin, and his facial expression was a sheer shock. Finally, he spoke.

"Damn, Baby girl. Be a kid. Enjoy being a kid. Go on vacations, travel, and enjoy life before becoming a parent," he urged, but it was too late. I already had a piece of my fiancé and I growing inside of me. Abortion was something many people suggested, but I could not abort my baby. Fuck how everyone felt. I was happy. I grew up and matured at a young age, and I felt strongly about keeping this baby and being a wonderful mother.

In June of 2009, I became a first-time mom, and nobody could tell me shit because I was super excited, and my baby girl was healthy and beautiful. I was in labor for 11 hours, and it was an unforgettable experience, as is everyone's birthing process. I had refused the epidural, out of fear of the huge needle going into my back. Needless to say, labor was painful, but I had some Tylenol and rode it out until the time came to push. The hospital staff broke my water, and the rest was history. I'm thankful that my partner, mother, and mother's sister were there to support me.

When my daughter was three months old, my boyfriend and I traveled to New York with our baby to meet my dad for the first time. I had her warmly dressed in a one-piece winter onesie and coat, and she looked extra sweet and cuddly. Despite my dad's advice to be a kid and wait for motherhood, he was elated when he saw my daughter. After all, she is his first grandchild. My father isn't a big crier, but he inched close to tears when he saw my daughter for the first time. He was joyful, and part of me believed this was my dad's second chance to be present in our lives, specifically present in my daughter's life, from childhood to adulthood, God willing.

My father missed so much throughout the years, and I felt his absence every day we were apart, especially as a new mom who needed her parents' love and support more than ever. As a new mom, regardless of age, your parents are the perfect examples to follow, seek trusted help, and provide emotional support, but my dad remained in New York, so there was very little he could do for his granddaughter and me.

I wasn't the only one affected by his absence, though.

His decision to run from the law caught up with him,

not in the legal sense, but emotionally speaking. Holidays passed, one by one, holidays he had spent alone and away from what he loves most in this world – his family. His baby girl, me, became a mother, and he was very happy, but it also hurt him to think if he had been around, I would have made different life choices. Also, he missed my daughter's milestones, and there were no amounts of photos or stories that could come close to experiencing her growth in person. Nevertheless, it was too late to dwell, especially on circumstances I could not change or the fact that I had a new role as a mother, but that didn't stop my father from feeling like shit for not being with me or being able to spend time with his grandchild to watch her grow. He kept his head up though because he knew this was the path he chose, and his actions had consequences.

With the bad comes the good, and although his emotions were often in disarray, he was making very good money working alongside various lawyers, despite his limited English. Ironically, my dad was well-respected among officers, detectives, judges, and lawyers, professionals he interacted with daily, the same professionals who spent countless hours searching for and prosecuting people on the run. To this day, the irony blows my mind. He walked freely into state and federal courtrooms and attended hearings in all five boroughs of New York City. Esteemed legal professionals had invited him to breakfast, lunch, and dinner, and he was among very powerful people. In a sense, his life had birthed a new beginning – a life involving a legal profession he was proud of, a life that allowed him to excel without selling drugs.

When you become a parent, all the issues and concerns that once occupied your mind soon become lesser priorities on the totem pole of life. So, although my father was always a concern of mine, and someone who will forever remain a high priority, I had a new life to raise and nurture. My focus had shifted, and my daughter became my number one priority.

My motherhood journey didn't stop there, though. In October of 2010, I became pregnant with our second daughter. This time around, my dad was happier because he liked my kids' father, and he saw the great job we were doing with our first daughter. I was working as a home health aide and my fiancé was an at-home tattoo artist. We were making it work but, of course, my dad thought we were still too young, yet he was extremely proud of our independence, stability, and healthy growing family.

That year was rather special in our lives. On September 3, 2010, my boyfriend became my fiancé. As our lives were going up, up, up, I knew I needed to attain an education and secure a job, so that our family could always be in a place of stability. Moreover, I wanted my children to grow up to value education and do the best they could in a classroom setting. I knew I needed to practice what I preach, which meant obtaining an education.

In June of 2011, after giving birth to my second daughter, I went back to school to acquire my GED, to which I graduated two months later. I was incredibly proud of myself. In a matter of two short months, especially having just given birth, I earned my GED, a feat that feels wonderful.

Two years later, I was pregnant with our third child. These pregnancies were planned, and I was excited because I always wanted a big family. Considering everything I went through as a child, I realized I wanted a large family to love, care for, and cherish. Importantly, I wanted a large family to teach and nurture to become loving, productive, wonderful humans in society.

That year, I went to visit my father, as I had been doing throughout the years, but this visit was a trip I won't ever forget. I was about seven months pregnant, and my father and I had just got off the BX11 bus. As we exited the bus, we began walking to my dad's cousin's house. The time was around 9 p.m., and the weather was a bit chilly. As my dad and I were walking and talking, per usual, I was telling him all the good gossip that had been going on back at home. During our father-daughter outings, we had so much to catch up on, and even if it was mindless gossip, I loved every second of these casual walks and talks. My dad was always a voice of reason, and I was waiting for the moment when I could tell him about managing my new life as a mother and fiancé. I was ready to unleash all my feelings that afternoon, and I figured who better to vent to than my dad.

As busy as New York City is, it seemed like he and I were the only ones on the sidewalk. He was hanging on my every word, and I enjoyed making my dad laugh and catching up on his chit chat. Those moments were precious, and I can't help but laugh because we were talking about the silliest stuff, yet this had such an impact on my life. As we were walking, I spotted a cop car driving down the street at an extremely slow pace. I began feeling nervous but tried not to show it.

"Papi, look at that cop. He's slowly coming towards us,"

I quietly told my dad.

"I already spotted him, Baby," he nonchalantly said.

I should've known my father's radar was already on. He may have been living a clean life, but he was still a fugitive who had to maintain that mindset in a sense.

The cop car slowly approached us, and we acted as if we didn't see it. I was walking close to the street, and my dad smoothly crossed in front of me and got on the side by the street. Suddenly, the cop turned on his light, not his sirens but his light, and pointed his bright flash toward us. I felt my heart fall to my ass. I was frightened and nervous, and I thought my water was going to break at that very moment.

"Hey!" the cop said as he finally reached us.

My dad slightly bent down, and in Spanish, he calmly said, "Yes?"

The cop replied, "Hey, buddy. You don't remember me?"

Then, my dad realized that he recognized him from the courthouse.

"What's up?" my dad asked in a friendly manner, obviously trying to deflect from any potential trouble.

Speaking Spanish, the officer asked my dad if he and I

needed a ride, and although the conversation was going smoothly, I stood there looking nervous, as if I stole something.

"No, thanks!" my dad politely declined. "We're only going around the corner."

"Okay! Have a great night," the cop said as he waved and drove off.

My dad and I just looked at each other and laughed because we both almost shit ourselves. There were plenty of times I've been in the courthouse with my dad and sat in court hearings with him, and every time I was a ball of nerves because I always thought someone would find out who my dad really was and there would be no way out, but thank God we were always okay.

Come to think of it, there were several crazy encounters, and each one left us feeling like our insides plummeted out of our bodies. Once, my father and sister were leaving the courthouse in Manhattan, as they were ready to grab some lunch during my father's lunch break. As they were walking, someone had said, "Don't move! Put your hands up!"

My sister had looked at my dad, and my dad told her to keep walking because he didn't think the officer was talking to them.

Then, my father and sister heard, "You with the black coat, walking with the girl, STOP!"

So, my dad and sister looked at each other, realizing the cop was, indeed, calling out to them, and as they turn around, the cop then says, "Come here."

The cop then spoke again, in Spanish. "Hey, friend! How have you been?! You remember me, right? I was just telling my friend that you are the best salsa dancer I know!"

They shared a good laugh, and then the officer wished him a great afternoon.

"I damn near had diarrhea running down my leg," said my dad to my sister later that evening as they recalled that crazy story.

***

No matter how much I had grown, and no matter how many times I visited New York, my dad always felt the same way when I boarded the bus to go back home. Knowing that I had to leave broke his heart and mine too. Even though my dad is a grown man, I wanted to stay with him and keep him safe. I guess that was part of my innate, motherly nature. I always wanted to care and protect the people I love.

As the years passed, I noticed that my dad's fingers had become deformed, almost like a monster's hands, because his gout was untreated for so long. His gout was starting to take a dramatic toll on his body. The uric acid was accumulating in his fingers, feet, knees, and elbows, and every time I visited him, his condition seemed to get worse. However, my dad could not receive medical treatment due to his status as a fugitive. I felt like shit seeing my dad like that, but I couldn't do anything about it. There were moments he would have a gout attack when his joints would become so swollen that he could barely walk, yet he always managed to smile and tell me he was okay.

My father's declining health, coupled with the random, messed-up parts of his job, made his life truly difficult. You see, my dad had a few lawyers play around with his money. Dad would land them cases, yet they would not pay him what he was promised. He would sit in the courthouse, from sunup to sundown, giving his cards to people coming out of court who needed lawyers. I hated that this was his life, but he had to do what he had to do to survive. When those lawyers would short-change him, Dad would be short on his rent, embarrassed to face the lady he was renting a room from because he knew he did not have her money. Dad was no longer at Grandma's house because his cousin was moving back. So, he began renting a room. My father would have to hide from his landlord to avoid having to tell her he didn't have the money. That made him feel like garbage. A man who had so much, wound up having nothing. People can say that is what he deserved, but my heart broke for him. No matter how sick he would feel or how much pain he was in, he always managed to make it to that courthouse because regardless of how he felt, he needed to eat and needed a place to sleep. I would always tell my dad to come home, but when I would go to the Berks' Most Wanted webpage and see his picture, I was reminded that my dad had no intention of coming back.

By 2016, I had my four children – three girls and one boy, and I had begun attending a two-year college, Berks Technical Institute, to pursue a degree in criminal justice. Ironically, I always wanted to be a lawyer. As a little girl, when my dad worked with lawyers, I was always with him, whether at hearings or a lawyer's office. I was intrigued by the fancy suits, the power, verbiage, and everything that encompassed this industry. Then, once my father got into the drug bullshit, the law interested me even more. I wanted to learn the ins and outs of our country's law system. So, I attended school for a few months but dropped out and decided to become a Certified Nurse Aide (CNA). At the time, I became discouraged and impatient by the entire process. I figured that my associate degree would have taken two years to complete versus three months of schooling to earn my CNA and begin making good money right away. I wasn't sure I could afford the two-year process when there was money waiting for me after three months of classes. In retrospect, I realize I had that quick-money mind frame, like my dad, because I set aside a loftier goal to go for the short-term, easier option and quicker money. However, my options were both legal, so while our circumstances were different, I realized I had that part of my dad within my spirit.

So, I went to a community college and earned my certificate in about three months. I was so proud of myself! The woman who once had no education was pursuing certifications and higher degrees. This was the example I wanted to set for my kids, and I knew it began with me. That same year, I decided that nursing wasn't exactly what I wanted to do for the rest of my life, so I decided to go back to BTI (Berks Technical Institute) and try my hand, yet again, at criminal justice. I discovered that they offered a paralegal degree, and I called my dad because that's right up his field.

"You would be great at this," he encouraged. "There's a lot of money to be made as a paralegal."

Despite being pregnant with my fourth child, I decided to go for it. My fiancé encouraged my goal, and I figured I'd give it my best shot. This entire situation must have been a sign from God because, as I started my classes, I fell in love with everything about the law field and learned a wealth of information. I realized that when something is meant for you, it feels good, and you don't have to struggle to attain it or keep it, education included.

One day in November, as I was sitting in class, something told me to pull up my dad's case. As I was learning new concepts and verbiage in school, I figured I would re-read Dad's case and try to interpret it from a more knowledgeable standpoint. When I pulled up his case, I realized all his open cases stated "closed." I was confused because during the other times I had checked, they always stated "open," but at this point, I understood legal terms and how to read these court documents. So, I opened the documents and discovered that Dad's cases had been nolle prossed.

I couldn't believe what I was seeing.

I sat at my desk in disbelief and confusion, but quickly snapped out of it when I realized I needed more details before fully understanding what this meant. I approached my teacher, someone who was an intelligent, experienced paralegal, and I asked her the meaning of a nolle prossed case.

"The case is closed," she explained, "but if the person were to ever get in trouble again, those cases can be reopened."

I quickly walked away, overcome with emotion. At that moment, my eyes welled up with tears, and I could not wait to go to my car to call my dad. When class ended, that's exactly what I did.

"Papi, are you sitting down?" I asked in excitement, barely able to contain myself.

"Yes, is everything okay?" he worriedly asked.

"Everything is fine, but are you sitting down?" I asked again. "I have some amazing news for you. Papi, are you ready for this? Your case is closed, Papi!" I shouted in excitement.

He seemed very confused by my news. "What do you

mean?" he said slowly, clearly confused by my admission.

I told him that I pulled up his case during class and learned that his case had been officially closed.

My dad quickly began talking to me in code words. "Oh, you mean they closed Coco's case?"

Coco is Dad's deceased brother, and we would always say "Coco" on the phone, in case the phones were being tapped.

"I'm telling you, Papi, it's okay to talk because your case is closed!"

"I'll have to look further into it and give you a call back later," he replied, completely caught off guard, seemingly skeptical of my news.

At this point, I knew I needed to get more facts on this because I easily understood why he was skeptical of my news. I immediately called the family-friend lawyer that my dad had worked with before he went on the run to tell him the good news of my findings and to ask for some advice. Although he could explain the terms and provide insight, he could not advise me because he was no longer practicing law. However, he did tell me to look further into it, and that's exactly what I did.

The following day, I went to the Berks County Clerk of Courts and pulled my dad's records. When I looked over his papers, one, in particular, stated the following:

And NOW, this 9th day of March 2016, I, the district attorney recommends and by virtue of the authority vested in me by law enter a Nolle Prosequi in the above-captioned matter. Reason: insufficient evidence. No activity since January of 2004 and NOW, this 10th day of March 2016 upon motion of the attorney for the Commonwealth it is hereby ORDERED that a Nolle Prosequi is entered in the above-captioned matter and if the defendant is held in custody solely on these charges and no other detainer then the defendant is to be discharged. It is further ordered that the county shall pay court costs.

Just like that, in knowing the truth and power of those words, my dad's case was over.

I was overcome with so many emotions. I shed tears of happiness in knowing that he was no longer wanted. My heart began racing because I imagined my dad living in the same town as us, no longer having to take the bus to New York to visit him for short weekends at a time. Life as I knew it was about to change, but this time for the better. We had memories to make and moments to seize, and I couldn't wait to get started.

That Friday, I went to school to print copies of all the papers from his case. After retrieving the papers, my fiancé and I boarded the next bus to New York, just so my father could have the proof in his hands.

I stepped off the bus and headed towards my father's apartment. I was filled with anticipation and excitement, as I was just a few minutes away from proving to my dad that he was a free man.

When I arrived at his place, my dad was in the middle of a prayer session. However, he didn't look too good. He wasn't feeling well, so before I shared the good news with him, we walked to the corner store for some garlic.

"When you eat a garlic clove, it helps decrease your blood pressure," he explained. I loved his fun facts and life hacks, and although I was full of excitement, I wanted to remain cautious of putting too much on my dad's plate while he felt sick.

Shortly after eating the clove of garlic, he felt much better. Finally, we decided to grab a bite to eat, and I was able to talk to him about the status of his freedom. I showed my father proof and he responded to my news with a blank stare.

"What's wrong, Dad?" I asked, concerned about the look on his face, confused that he wasn't jumping for joy. I expected elation. I expected tears, shouting, and jumping with joy.

"Oh, I'm fine, Baby. I'm just thinking," he said calmly with a half-smile, seemingly in disbelief.

"You're a free man, Dad," I said, giving him a huge smile and his hands a squeeze.

Later that evening, my fiancé, dad, sister, and I went to BBQs in the Bronx to eat, drink, and celebrate. I truly believe that God put the desire in my heart to go back to school, so I could be the one to crack that case open and let him know he was a free man. Even though he knew it was true, he wasn't looking to go back to his former shithole of a city. Reading is my home, but Reading is a small city with absolutely nothing to do. The city is overpopulated with not nearly enough jobs for its people, and it lacks any life or safe entertainment for kids. New York, on the other hand, has opportunities around every corner, 24/7, and the options for life and entertainment are endless. I don't blame him for not wanting to return to

Reading. I mean, we were in Reading, but we also visited my dad quite often, so I wasn't exactly upset when he didn't jump at the chance to move back to our bleak city. Through the lens of my 11-year-old eyes, moving back to Reading was the best idea. However, when thinking about this situation with a sound frame of mind, New York City was certainly the best place for my father to reside and work, despite the distance between us.

In 2017, my fiancé and I got pregnant with baby number five, another baby boy, and we were happy as could be with our squad of seven. My dad couldn't believe the news.

"Dammit, don't you have a TV, a book to read, or Wi-Fi in your house?" he jokingly asked as he laughed and congratulated me.

My father was so happy that he was going to be a grandfather again. This time, he had the freedom to be more present in his grandchildren's lives.

CHAPTER SEVEN

"We must be free not because we claim freedom, but because we practice it."

– William Faulkner

My dad was thrilled to know he was officially a free man, but he remained guarded. Although he was a free man, there wasn't a sudden, drastic change in him or within his life. After all, he had been living his life on the outside of a jail cell, yet he was restricted from having to change his identity and lifestyle drastically. So much time had passed, and with time came adjustment. Somehow, my dad got used to his new life, so when freedom was within reach, he didn't exactly feel like a new person. There wasn't some "ah-ha" moment of freedom and glory that you may imagine one feels when their charges are no longer pending. However, I did notice a shift in my father's mindset. I noticed a new pep in his step. He walked with his head held high, and he looked forward to every morning, viewing his days as new, fresh starts. Truth be told, my father's heart would still skip a beat at the sudden sight of an officer, but he would silently remind himself that he was a free man and didn't have to feel uncomfortable.

"Are you sure I'm good?" my father would occasionally ask me, obviously still fearful that someone would arrest him.

In those moments, I realized that my dad didn't pay the price in prison, yet his price tag came at the cost of peace and contentment. Always looking over your shoulder is no way to live, and since old habits die hard, it was hard for my dad to accept and process that he was free.

"Let's all go on vacation!" I would urge, and he would enthusiastically agree, but only to make me happy at that moment because we knew he wasn't going anywhere. I could see in his face that he wasn't ready to come home or venture elsewhere and face his long-time fear of ultimately being arrested for a crime he committed years ago. So, even though he had all the proof he needed, he still felt the fear of detectives coming to arrest him.

Despite his fear, my dad continued his life as it had been for the past several years, but with his head held higher and his dreams feeling more attainable. At this point, my father's goal was to reunite with his family and catch up on missed time. He couldn't make up for lost time, but he knew he could create new memories going forward. He also wanted to start making more money with local lawyers.

That year, my dad was awarded a pay increase, earning 40% of each case he brought to the lawyers, and he set his sights on attaining more cases for more attorneys. My dad was always a hustler, and I had faith in him that he could increase his earning power, especially now that he had more confidence.

My dad may have had goals, but his dreams of spending more time with his family remained just that – a dream. My dad remained afraid to leave New York. He made a million and one excuses as to why he couldn't visit or meet somewhere else. I wanted him to come to Pennsylvania, which was hardly a long ride from New York so that he could spend time with my family and I, but that never happened. So, we continued going back and forth to New York to visit him.

My mom was thrilled that his case was finally over;

however, they were no longer a couple. When my dad left for New York, ultimately leaving my mom behind, my mom held on to hope that things would blow over and we could be a family again, but after days, months, and years passed, she opened her eyes to the fact that they could no longer have a relationship. They had never married, but their relationship was over. Despite their failed romance, they remain great friends to this day. Her love for him runs deep, but no longer as her partner, only as the father of her daughter.

As for my dad and his dating life, I never saw a woman in his life, let alone heard of one. If he did have a relationship, he kept it on the hush, but I don't think he wanted to be with anyone. He never expected my mom to wait for him, but I'm sure he wished they could have stayed together. Impossible, I know, but that's the way their story unfolded. My mother dated after my father, but my dad wasn't upset. I mean, what could he do, right? His actions had consequences, as he once told me long ago, and that included losing my mother.

Currently, my father still works for lawyers because he loves what he does for a living. That's one aspect of his life that hasn't failed or gone awry, and I'm happy for him because it's honest work and something he enjoys. When you enjoy what you do, your life feels meaningful. You don't dread waking up each morning to head to work, and I couldn't be happier that my dad went from hustling in the streets to hustling in the courtroom. My father has been away from the drug game for so long that he never wants that drug dealing life again because with fast money came a lot of emptiness, fear, trouble, and bullshit. Money isn't everything, because if it were, he would've stayed in the game and continued risking it all.

Sure, money can buy you a home, a really big home, but it can't buy you happiness within the home. With money comes relationship problems, too, and not just involving one's love life, although money confused my father's love life with my mom. When you're rich, you suddenly have more friends than what you're used to, yet you're unsure which friends are genuine and which are using you for convenience and perks. My father had a lot of "friends" who owed him money and a lot of friends that stole from him on the low. With money and fake friends also came fear. Fear because you don't know who will turn on you or bust down your door at 5 am, whether the police or someone trying to rob you. Money simply can't buy peace.

My father has not traveled yet, but we have plans to go to Puerto Rico to visit his parents and sister. He hasn't seen his parents in years, but he speaks to them all the time on the phone. Speaking on the phone and seeing someone in person is completely different, and it's time for my dad to feel that in-person love and connection with his parents. I wonder how this will feel for him, and I hope he is overcome with love instead of anxiety and fear. He deserves to enjoy this soon-to-be beautiful moment.

At one point, I hoped my dad wouldn't develop any social anxiety or shyness because he ran from the law for so long, but I realized he never developed deep-seated social anxiety because he walked the streets of New York and was generally friendly to everyone he came in contact with. Yes, he looked over his shoulder, but he also enjoyed carrying a conversation with others, whether you were the mayor or a homeless person. He is a people-person, and although he lived a quiet life, his personality was still larger than life.

As for his faux identity, most people in New York know him by his alias, so they continue to call him by that name. Plus, he doesn't feel the need to explain his situation to anyone. At home, however, everyone calls him by his real name, which I know he's still getting used to. To think that my father is re-adjusting to someone calling him by his birth name still blows me away, because that was the name he came into this world with, yet after so much time of being called another name, I suppose he mentally transitioned, and that takes time to process. Nevertheless, my father is a much happier person now that he doesn't have to hide his identity. Understandably, a weight has been lifted, but when someone has looked over their shoulder for years, that doesn't automatically stop once their freedom has been granted. Physical freedom is easier to adjust to as opposed to mental freedom. My dad was still shackled, mentally speaking. Like a person behind bars who was released after years of imprisonment, my father had some adjusting to do, and he wasn't the only one who had to cope with emotional and mental changes. I had uphill battles of my own.

CHAPTER EIGHT

"Every time you are tempted to react in the same old way, ask if you want to be a prisoner of the past or a pioneer of the future."

– Deepak Chopra

My dad's freedom didn't suddenly change everything in our lives, especially not mine. Our lives didn't magically go back to normal. I'm not even sure we had a strong grasp on the meaning of "normal," because our lives were always unconventional in one way or another. The way my father unexpectedly left my life, physically speaking, caused many issues that only deepened with time, namely PTSD and anxiety.

Currently, I'm working on finding inner peace due to my battle with post-traumatic stress disorder (PTSD), anxiety, and panic attacks. There isn't a quick fix to taming one's PTSD.

However, I find peace when listening to motivational speeches, attending yoga classes, and writing and reciting affirmations. When I focus on mindfulness and expressing gratitude, my sense of joy deepens, and that is one of my greatest focuses right now. Working on being a sounder, happier, better me involves patience and self-love, and I try to take life hour by hour, rather than pressuring myself to feel better immediately.

My father's sudden departure wasn't the only reason for my PTSD. From the time I was six years old, up until I was ten, I was molested. Since then, I've suffered from PTSD, which spawned anxiety and panic attacks.

The abuse led me to feel disgusted with myself, and I never told anyone about this besides my confidant, my sister. Child abusers often manipulate their victims into feeling disgusted and shameful, often targeting children, as they know children are easily susceptible to feelings of guilt and fear of getting in trouble. Nevertheless, I told my sister long ago. She knows everything about me, and I felt safe telling her my secret. In turn, she told me she was also molested, and that was a commonality I never wanted to share with her. Eventually, I also told my fiancé, and I feel great comfort and strength with his support and protection.

Despite my dad's ordeal with the police and his former life in the streets, I firmly believe that my emotional turmoil is not my parents' fault. The truth is, my sister and I experienced some fucked up shit that was part of our journey, and these situations, although traumatic, molded my sister and I into intelligent, street-smart, book-smart survivors. My sister and I turned out to be completely different, but that's what makes us unique. Even though we encountered a lot of the same battles, we are still standing, ten toes down and strong. Truth be told, even if my dad never ran from the police, I still do not believe he could have protected my sister and I from being molested. My dad, although wise, loving, and powerful, could not be everywhere at once, whether he ran from the law or not, and that included the moments I was abused.

Although I was molested at a young age, my feelings festered and lingered, and my first panic attack did not happen until I was about 19 years old. For those who don't know, the physical effects of anxiety and panic attacks are out of this world. They hit you like a ton of bricks, usually out of nowhere, and you have very little control over how to make these go away as quickly as they started. During my first attack, I happened to be driving and felt my throat tighten. I'm not sure what triggered this attack, but something must have sparked something inside that made me feel this way. I started to hyperventilate, my heart pounded uncontrollably, and I wanted to get out of my car and run, scream, and cry. I felt like I was going to die because these feelings overwhelmed me in a way that seemed never-ending and paralyzing. Not knowing what the hell was happening to me, I went home, turned on my child's asthma machine, and did an asthma treatment in hopes this incident was asthma-related. After about 15 minutes of the asthma treatments, my body and mind calmed down and I was "better." I didn't know whether I had a breathing issue or another health problem. I felt near-death and was finally relieved to calm down and return to a normal state of breathing.

After several more anxiety attacks, I finally went to a therapist because I knew this wasn't normal, and I started to feel as if my issue was mental and emotional. Eventually, I was diagnosed with PTSD, anxiety, and panic disorder. With that said, in knowing my diagnosis, I know that my mind is always in fight-or-flight mode. I overthink everything and worry way more than I should. I live my everyday life thinking something is wrong with me or is going to go wrong. I am always super aware of my children's every move because of what happened to me as a child. I wish I could keep my precious children in a bubble, but since I can't, the uncontrollable parts of my life add to my anxiety. During playdates with other children, I watch my kids like a hawk, and every little interaction sparks panic because I worry that it could lead to something harmful. Even when we are among family, I keep a close eye on my children because I can't seem to trust anyone. What some people find enjoyable, such as playdates and family outings, I see as dreadful because this means I need to be a hover mother. I don't "need" to be a hover mother, but I do not feel safe for my children, otherwise. In working on inner peace and reaching a place of genuine healing, I realize I can't live this way. However, moving past these fears is taking some time.

What I have learned, however, is that happiness means enjoying the little things such as waking up with my children and fiancé every day, because my dad could have only wished to do things like that for all the years he was gone, and this is a beautiful blessing I enjoy. In fact, I realize that isn't a "little thing," as some people aren't afforded those opportunities.

I haven't fully achieved joy, but I do know that happiness is getting to be whoever you want and not allowing your past to dictate your future. At times, I feel ashamed that I allow my fears to control me, but every day, I take the initiative to create a better me for me. I work on trying not to pick my brain so that I can learn to control my emotions and not allow my feelings to control me. In doing so, I listen to motivational and personal development speeches every day on YouTube. Some of my favorites are Les Brown, The Anxiety Guy, Be Inspired, Blessed and Unstoppable, Et The Hip Hop Preacher, and Fearless Soul. I am currently practicing yoga, which I love more than rigorous workouts at the gym. Yoga is deeply personal. The quiet time, stretches, and deep breathing allow me to come to a place filled with positive energy. There's no body-shaming in those classes, either. Despite being half-naked or in tight clothing, people are concentrated on mental, emotional, and physical elevation, and I believe yoga is a beautiful gateway to reaching emotional freedom.

Not only do I find solace with yoga and other solo activities, but I feel immense peace and joy when spending time with loved ones, especially my partner. With my fiancé by my side, I can conquer anything. He is the salt to my pepper and peanut butter to my jelly. All clichés aside, he is amazing. We have our ups and downs, as every couple experiences, but if there is such a thing as perfect, he is damn near that. When I have anxiety to the point of losing sleep, and my heart is pounding, I can't breathe, I have tingling in my body, and my stomach is so upset that I'm shitting all night or can't eat, he holds me on his lap and rocks me as if I were a baby. This may seem strange or even funny, but you can only laugh if you've never experienced it because anxiety is no joking matter. I also believe that this is the way my fiancé knows how to provide comfort for me because he does not exactly understand my anxiety. Despite not relating to my anxiety, he does everything in his power to give me confidence and ease my fears. His love amazes me, and I'm moved by his commitment to helping me, even when he isn't sure how to go about that.

Throughout this unique and sometimes painful journey, I am learning to love myself. In learning this priceless lesson, I encourage you to enjoy being you. We are born unique. Choose to stand out because you were not meant to blend with the crowd. No matter what I've been through, I know I am a great mother and fiancé and an amazing person with a fabulous personality. I am intelligent, and I love hard. I'm not quite sure what my purpose is in life just yet, but I'm pretty sure when I find it, it will slap me in the face as if to say, "I've been here all along, and you didn't see me!"

I love that if I really want something, I will go after it by any means necessary. No matter how scared I may be, I always force myself to build the courage to do it because I am a firm believer that everything you'll ever want is on the other side of fear, and that is why I keep pushing – because I know I will conquer these demons and on the other side of this pain is joy. I will be a victor, no longer a victim.

Inner peace, for me, is living in the moment and not the past. Living in the past makes you fear the future, and living in the future will have you anxious and overthinking every little thing. So, I encourage you to live in the moment and leave everything in God's hands, or whoever you believe in, and hold on to faith.

Hold on to your faith, even when life seems bleak. I pray every morning and thank God for another day of life, not only for myself but also for those I love deeply. God has done many beautiful things for me and mine. He never lets me stay down. I may trip, stumble, and fall, but He always lifts me back up. I know that I am a strong woman, but my strength is on account of God and my prayer life. There is no possible way I could overcome this wild ride without the help of our Lord and Savior.

In my prayer life, I am able to share gratitude, and in sharing gratitude, I feel joy. I pray for forgiveness, for I am human and commit sins. I pray for my health and thank God for another day above ground, as I have my five senses and healthy limbs. I thank him for the incredible milestones I've reached, mentally, professionally, and emotionally, and I pray that He continues to bless everything I put my hands on. We serve a glorious God, and I'm thankful to experience His grace and mercy.

Unveiling layers of myself, sharing my father's journey, and coming to grips with my truths, even the painful truths, allows for growth and the creation of new strengths. I encourage you to speak your beautiful life into existence. Affirm yourself. Feed yourself beautiful words. You deserve them. Each morning, I look at myself in my bathroom mirror and speak love.

I am loved.

I am smart, beautiful, and loving.

I am a successful entrepreneur.

I am a child of God.

I am a wonderful fiancé, mother, daughter, sister, aunt, and friend.

I also affirm my children, too. My words are food to their soul, and it's best to nourish them with positivity and love. Every day, I tell my children that they are beautiful, inside and out. I ask that they thank God for allowing them to see another day. I tell them they are special stars that shine bright and have bright futures ahead, too.

As humans, we tend to take little things for granted, like enjoying a family-filled Sunday movie night, waking up in our bed, and seeing the faces of the people we love. Those are fortunes my dad lost when he lived a life on the run. As significant as his decision was to run and how this decision affected my life, I now choose to focus on the present, and I am happy to have him with us as a free man. Sharing these personal experiences is not to boast about my dad escaping the system but to share how our lives unfolded because of our choices. My father didn't pay his consequences in prison, but the universe made him pay. In turn, I preach to my children about the importance of wise decision-making and how their actions have consequences. I will use my journey and my father's journey as lessons, and those lessons will help me raise my children to be intelligent, mindful people who are not driven by fear, guilt, greed, or materialism.

CHAPTER NINE

"What is a man? He is a father, a husband, a son, a brother, a
friend; he is everything that one needs in life. He runs the house,
he is the hero in the house, a boss, an employee."

– Unknown

In July of 2018, my dad was sitting in his friend's barbershop in New York, where he spent time, every day, for the past 13 years, when he said to have felt a weird feeling in his chest. So, he drank some water, but the feeling didn't go away. It was a feeling he hadn't felt before.

"Fuck this," he finally said. "I need to get to a doctor."

So, his friend's niece took him to the nearest emergency room, only to discover that he had a mini heart attack. When my sister called me to tell me the news, who had found out from my father's friend, I was devastated and in disbelief. I immediately began to pray because that's all I could do at the moment.

Later that day, my dad called me and told me that he was okay and felt much better, but he explained that he had a small blockage in his heart, and the doctors wanted to operate. My father opposed their suggestion because he wanted a second opinion at a different hospital. My father claimed he wanted a second opinion, which is common when receiving a diagnosis, but I know my dad was petrified and avoiding the truth about his health issues. I knew he was scared, but I cried to him and begged him to let the doctors do what they had to do. He ended up calling me the next day, telling me he was going to let them put a stent in his heart, and so the process began.

During his hospital stay, my dad found out he had type-2 diabetes, high blood pressure, and a four-centimeter spot on the bottom of his left lung. Whether these conditions were hereditary, I'm not sure, but that was his diagnosis and we knew he needed to do his part to change his health. It also didn't help that he hadn't visited a doctor in years. Had he received regular checkups, I imagine this could have been avoided or detected earlier. Nevertheless, we couldn't go back in time, only adjust to the present.

The doctors were not sure what the spot was and wanted to do further testing. Two days later, me, my little brother, and two of my daughters went to New York to visit my dad. My heart ached from seeing my dad in those conditions, but he managed to tell me he was okay, as usual. I spoke to the doctor when I got there, and she told me he was doing much better with the stent in his heart. She also explained that they were going to refer my father to a specialist for the spot on his lung. The doctor then said she was going to refer him to various specialists and that she planned to send him to rehab to increase his strength. During his hospital stay, he felt extremely weak, and rehab was now necessary.

As I looked around the hospital that day, I started to feel irritated. The facility was filthy, and the staff was working my nerves. The bathroom sink was covered in hair that did not belong to my father. The toilet hadn't been cleaned, either. Worse, the staff was very rude when I asked questions regarding my dad's health. His condition was foreign to me, and I had a few questions on my mind, but their coldness and rudeness provided very little insight into the thoughts on my mind. All I could think is that I needed to get him the hell out of there. I left New York the next day, and before I left, my father was trying to act normally, as if he was 100% fine, but he wasn't and we could tell, but like any reassuring father, he didn't want us to worry. He had my sister with him, and he had family and friends coming by to visit and bring him food, so while I was grateful he was in good company, I wished I could be by his side, too. Driving back to Pennsylvania, I kept thinking about getting my dad back home with me because I believed that if I left him in New York, he would die. He wasn't eating right and was losing weight by the day. He had said the hospital food was disgusting, and I believe his stomach was shrinking because when the family would bring him food, he wasn't eating that either. It was as if his appetite was gone and his taste buds were nonexistent.

When I arrived home in Reading, I called my father and asked him if he would like to come to Reading so I could take care of him. Surprisingly, he said he would think about it. His answer was far better than a flat out "no," so I hoped he would take me up on my offer. The thought of him and his poor state of health made me cry. Worse, seeing him skinny and sickly was heartbreaking.

Once he was released from the hospital, he went back to the emergency room because he felt pain in his chest. In retrospect, I believe he was afraid of becoming sicker, so he preferred to be admitted to the hospital rather than be at home. Plus, my father owed rent, and it kept increasing as the days passed. He was out of work due to being sick and life was getting hard for him. When he was home, before his hospital admittance, he would merely stay in his room, letting himself waste away, not eating and not checking his blood sugar levels because he couldn't use his machine due to his enlarged fingers from gout. All around, my father was deeply stressed, fatigued, and deteriorating.

In early September, the hospital sent my father to rehab, so my sister met with him and went to the facility to check it out. They both told me it was disgusting. They turned around, left, and didn't look back. I couldn't take this shit anymore. Between the awful facilities and careless staff, I was at my wit's end. So, I called my father on September 11th and flatly said, "I'm coming for you. Enough is enough."

"Let me get some things in order, and you can come to get me," he replied.

I agreed to give him just a bit of time, but the following

day, my father remained undecided. Despite his uncertainty, I made an executive decision to pick him up.

"No! I'm coming for you tomorrow. I'm not going to let you die all alone," I demanded, putting my foot down and refusing to take "no" for an answer.

My father actually agreed. "You're right," he said. "Come tomorrow."

On September 13th, I drove to New York to pick up my dad. My baby brother came with me, and we met with my sister at my dad's place to pack up his stuff. Within a few hours, we were ready to go. My heart was in a million pieces when I saw him. He was wearing a T-shirt with some sweatpants and sneakers, all of which didn't fit him. My father never has, and I mean never, worn ill-fitting, tattered clothing. He had always been suited up, no matter how he felt. On this day, though, he was so unkempt and emaciated. My dad usually weighed around 200 pounds, but when I picked him up in New York that day, he was down to about 140 pounds. I really couldn't believe my eyes.

Before leaving New York, we went to the pharmacy to pick up any medicine he had there, and as we made our way to retrieve his prescriptions, I noticed the sad look on my father's face. I knew he had a lot going on in his head, so I tried to let him process his feelings and thoughts without interfering. After all, my father was leaving the city he had been content in for the last 17 years. He was feeling sick and weak, and he was about to face a new reality and painful past because he was heading back to the place where all the bullshit began – Reading, Pennsylvania.

Before this trip to NYC, Mom and I agreed that I would do what I have to for him, such as make his doctor appointments and handle whatever errands he needed, and she would have him stay at her house. My father didn't want to stay at my house because he felt like a burden, even though he wouldn't have been one, but he looked at the situation as if I had enough going on with my fiancé and kids.

When we got back to Reading, my Dad wanted to lay down. He was exhausted from the trip. Although short, it was more movement than he's done in quite some time. The next day, I went to my mom's house to visit him, and he wasn't up for doing much, but I also caught on to the fact that he didn't want to be seen. Emotionally and mentally, he wasn't ready for all of that, and I respected his feelings. Plus, he didn't want others to see him this way. September 19th, a few days later, was his birthday. So, I picked him up and we went to Red Lobster for dinner. My father was elated because he hadn't been there in years. Not only was he happy, but I was overjoyed, too. Taking my father out for his birthday felt incredible. No hiding, no fake names, no rushing to leave, and momentarily shedding any shame of his new figure, we enjoyed every moment. We basked in our time together, and while that may not sound like much to some, that evening was special for us because this was the first birthday in years that I got to spend with him. After dinner, we went to my house to enjoy cake. My fiancé, children, and I cut him a slice of cake, and you could see the pure joy in his eyes. After what seemed like ages of feeling physically and emotionally awful, Dad wholeheartedly enjoyed that evening and felt a surge of energy.

At this point in the evening, I was trying to get my father to ease up more in terms of leaving the house and seeing the beauty in not staying indoors all the time. I pointed out that if I had left it up to him, he would have stayed in the house and hid from the world. Whether he was uncomfortable with his appearance or apprehensive about starting over in his old town, I'm unsure, but I was there to have his back through thick and thin. Growing up, we often hear, "It's what's on the inside that counts," and this couldn't be truer. My dad's appearance was changing, and his health was declining, yet the man I loved with a heart of gold was standing in front of me, on his birthday, and there was nothing more beautiful than that.

Within the coming days, I started scheduling my father's doctor appointments and other necessary appointments, so that he could receive insurance and see local doctors regarding his diabetes, high blood pressure, and gout. Also, we needed to get him a new residency card, which was a process because it took so long, but thank God, everything went smoothly, without anything from his past creeping up. Thankfully, the insurance process and setting doctor appointments fell into place quickly. At one point, though, his schedule got a bit crazy because he was loaded with appointments and, of course, I had to make sure he got there, which I managed to do with some help from my mom. My father was referred to a heart doctor and rheumatologist which was great because I wanted to make sure what happened in New York wasn't going to repeat itself.

When I took him to his first appointment with his new

doctor, they said his heart sounded great and the blockage he had did not cause permanent damage. We were incredibly grateful. This news was music to our ears.

On November 6, 2018, I gave birth to my fifth child, my second son. My dad was thrilled because this was the first child of mine that he was able to enjoy since birth, although he was scared to hold him because my son was a small baby – five pounds and 14 ounces. On November 9th, I turned 27 years old, and although I was still in pain from giving birth, my birthday was incredible because my dad was there to spend my day with me. For years, this is all I wanted, and the moment had finally arrived. A few days later, Thanksgiving rolled around, and shortly after that, Christmas. Finally, a full holiday season with the ones I loved, no longer going from city to city to end with tearful goodbyes. Talk about all my prayers answered.

CHAPTER TEN

"In our daily lives, we must see that it is not happiness that makes us grateful, but the gratefulness that makes us happy."
– Albert Clarke

Today, thank God, my father is back to weighing about 190 pounds, dancing salsa, and busting down those moves. His health has improved drastically, and he looks amazing. Here and there, he faces minor health-related setbacks but nothing like before. His diabetes is fairly under control, his gout is being treated, and he is no longer required to take medication for his heart.

My father looks at life differently now. He enjoys being

around his grandchildren, often telling me they give him life. We do things as a family, such as staying in hotels to enjoy the pool during the cold weather and taking the kids to the dairy farm to feed the animals and eat ice cream. In a way, having him in Reading, especially with my kids, makes up for the time he missed with my siblings and I. I enjoy watching him walk into church with my three daughters, the same church we attended when I was a kid. It appears as though life is repeating itself when I see my father and babies walk into church. This is such a beautiful feeling, just seeing him walk, because there was a time when he could barely move. Now, he's walking with my kids, attending services, and praising the Lord. What a mighty God we serve.

The life I once knew as a child is long gone, and although the memories remain and I continue to work through various emotions and thoughts, I choose to use those experiences for good – for my good, my partner's good, and my children's good. Perspective is key. I can view my father's decisions as hindrances, or I can look for the blessings in the lessons, and the latter is what I intend to do. My dad's story belongs to him but I have taken his journey and used it to propel mine in creating a family I am proud of, establishing a career I enjoy, and making beautiful memories to far surpass my life.